foreword

Who doesn't love pizza? It's simple, quick and so tasty! And it's versatile. The crust is basically a blank canvas waiting to be decorated with an array of fresh, mouthwatering ingredients. When it comes to toppings, the possibilities are endless. And the variety of crusts available to the pizza connoisseur is impressive. In fact, there are so many options that it can be a bit mind-boggling trying to figure out what to choose.

Don't worry—we are here to help. We've compiled some of our favourite pizza recipes to help you navigate the pizza landscape: traditional favourites—deep dish, thin crust, stuffed crust—and some unconventional pizzas you and your family will love—quinoa pizza, anyone? Whether you are a carnivore, vegetarian or somewhere in between, you'll find something to love in these pages.

basic pizza crust dough with simple pizza sauce

A crispy, lightly browned crust with a bread-like texture, and a classic pizza sauce. Add your choice of toppings and enjoy!

CRUST

Warm water	3/4 cup	175 mL
Granulated sugar	1/2 tsp.	2 mL
Active dry yeast	2 tsp.	10 mL
All-purpose flour	2 cups	500 mL
Salt	1 1/2 tsp.	7 mL
Olive (or cooking) oil	2 tbsp.	30 mL

SAUCE

Olive (or cooking) oil	1 tbsp.	15 mL
Chopped onion	1 cup	250 mL
Garlic clove, minced	1	1
Diced canned tomatoes, with juice (19 oz., 540 mL)	1	1
Tomato paste (5 1/2 oz., 156 mL)	1	1
Dried basil	1/2 tsp.	2 mL
Dried oregano	1/4 tsp.	1 mL
Salt	1/2 tsp.	2 mL
Pepper	1/8 tsp.	0.5 mL
Granulated sugar	1 tsp.	5 mL

Crust: Stir warm water and sugar in small bowl until sugar is dissolved. Sprinkle yeast over top. Let stand for 10 minutes. Stir until yeast is dissolved.

Combine flour and salt in large bowl. Add yeast mixture and olive oil. Mix until dough pulls away from side of bowl and is no longer sticky, adding a little more flour if necessary. Turn dough out onto lightly floured surface. Knead for 5 to 10 minutes until smooth and elastic. Place dough in greased large bowl, turning once to grease top. Cover with greased plastic wrap and tea towel. Let stand in oven with light on and door closed for about 1 hour until doubled in size. Turn dough out onto lightly floured surface. Shape into ball. Makes one 12 inch (30 cm) pizza crust. See Tip, page 64.

Sauce: Heat olive oil in large saucepan. Add onion and garlic. Sauté until soft.

Add next 7 ingredients. Heat, stirring often, until boiling. Boil gently for about 15 minutes. Makes about 3 cups (750 mL).

1/6 of crust with sauce: 250 Calories; 7 g Total Fat (5 g Mono, 0.6 g Poly, 0.7 g Sat); 0 mg Cholesterol; 40 g Carbohydrate; 1 g Fibre; 6 g Protein; 1060 mg Sodium

guacamole pizza

Nippy and flavourful, this pizza tastes best with a white-floured crust. The topping can be made ahead and refrigerated, and the crust can also be crisped ahead. Assemble just before serving.

Partially baked 12 inch (30 cm) pizza	1	1
Ripe avocados, peeled and mashed	2	2
Lemon juice	2 tbsp.	30 mL
Minced onion flakes	1 tbsp.	15 mL
Salt	1/2 tsp.	2 mL
Garlic powder	1/4 tsp.	1 mL
Hot pepper sauce	1/4 tsp.	1 mL
Medium tomato, diced	1	1
Grated sharp Cheddar cheese	1/2 cup	125 mL

Place partially baked crust directly on bottom rack in 400°F (200°C) oven. Bake for 2 minutes. Turn crust over. Bake for 2 minutes. Cool.

Mash avocado and lemon juice together. Add next 4 ingredients. Mash together. Gently fold in tomato. Spread over crust.

Sprinkle with cheese. Cuts into 20 wedges.

1 wedge: 100 Calories; 5 g Total Fat (3 g Mono, 0.5 g Poly, 1 g Sat); <5 mg Cholesterol; 12 g Carbohydrate; 2 g Fibre; 3 g Protein; 250 mg Sodium

bruschetta pizza

An attractive twist to the usual bruschetta. Colourful with flavour to match.

Basic pizza crust dough, page 2

Salad dressing (or mayonnaise)	1/2 cup	125 mL
Grated Parmesan cheese	1/4 cup	60 mL
Dried oregano	1 tsp.	5 mL
Dried basil	1/2 tsp.	2 mL
Pepper	1/2 tsp.	2 mL
Garlic cloves, minced	2	2
Chopped pitted ripe olives	1/3 cup	75 mL
Plum tomatoes, seeded and diced	3	3
Grated part-skim mozzarella cheese	1 1/2 cups	375 mL

Roll dough out on lightly floured surface. Press in greased 12 inch (30 cm) pizza pan or 9 x 13 inch (23 x 33 cm) pan. Poke holes all over crust, except edge, with fork. Bake on bottom rack in 425°F (220°C) oven for 8 minutes. Press down any bulges. Cool slightly.

Combine next 6 ingredients in medium bowl. Spread over crust.

Sprinkle with olives, tomato and mozzarella cheese. Bake for about 8 minutes. Cuts into 16 long, thin appetizer wedges or 24 squares.

***1 wedge:** 170 Calories; 10 g Total Fat (5 g Mono, 2 g Poly, 2.5 g Sat); 10 mg Cholesterol; 13 g Carbohydrate; <1 g Fibre; 5 g Protein; 380 mg Sodium*

nacho pizza

Can't decide between nachos or pizza? You don't have to with this creative dish—two favourite snack foods rolled into one! Best served hot.

Refrigerator crescent-style rolls (8 per tube)	8 oz.	235 g
Canned jalapeño bean dip	2/3 cup	150 mL
Onion salt	1/8 tsp.	0.5 mL
Garlic salt	1/8 tsp.	0.5 mL
Cayenne pepper	1/8 tsp.	0.5 mL
Grated medium Cheddar cheese	1 cup	250 mL
Broken corn chips	2/3 cup	150 mL
Seeded and diced tomato	1/2 cup	125 mL
Chopped green onion	1/4 cup	60 mL
Grated medium Cheddar cheese	1 cup	250 mL

Unroll dough. Press to fit in greased 12 inch (30 cm) pizza pan. Press seams together, forming rim around edge. Bake in 375°F (190°C) oven for about 6 minutes until just turning golden. Cool.

Mash bean dip, onion salt, garlic salt and cayenne pepper together in small bowl. Spread over crust.

Sprinkle with first amount of cheese and corn chips. Scatter tomato, green onion and second amount of cheese over top. Return to oven. Bake for 10 minutes. Serve warm. Cuts into 16 wedges.

1 wedge: 130 Calories; 8 g Total Fat (1.5 g Mono, 0 g Poly, 4 g Sat); 15 mg Cholesterol; 8 g Carbohydrate; <1 g Fibre; 5 g Protein; 290 mg Sodium

tortilla pizza wedges

Start with flour tortillas and basil pesto, and you've got tempting, pizza-like wedges in under half an hour.

Basil pesto	3 tbsp.	45 mL
Flour tortillas (9 inch, 23 cm, diameter)	2	2
Sliced fresh white mushrooms	1/2 cup	125 mL
Chopped red pepper	1/4 cup	60 mL
Sliced green onion	2 tbsp.	30 mL
Grated Italian cheese blend	1 cup	250 mL

Spread pesto over tortillas, almost to edge. Place, pesto side up, on greased baking sheet.

Scatter next 3 ingredients over pesto.

Sprinkle with cheese. Bake in 450°F (230°C) oven for about 8 minutes until cheese is melted and tortillas are golden. Let stand on pan for 1 minute. Makes 20 wedges.

__1 wedge:__ 43 Calories; 2.1 g Total Fat (0 g Mono, 0 g Poly, 0.5 g Sat); 2 mg Cholesterol; 4 g Carbohydrate; trace Fibre; 2 g Protein; 109 mg Sodium

pumpkin pizza wedges

*The jack-o'-lantern jumps into the pizza pan for these cheesy wedges!
These could serve as a fabulously grown-up Halloween appetizer, their fall
flavours of fresh sage and pumpkin pairing well with a full-bodied red wine.*

Butter (or hard margarine)	1 tbsp.	15 mL
Cooking oil	1 tbsp.	15 mL
Thinly sliced onion	2 cups	500 mL
Salt	1/4 tsp.	1 mL
Pepper	1/8 tsp.	0.5 mL
Canned pure pumpkin (no spices), see Tip, page 64	1 cup	250 mL
Chopped fresh sage (or 3/4 tsp., 4 mL, dried)	1 tbsp.	15 mL
Prebaked pizza crust (12 inch, 30 cm, diameter)	1	1
Grated Asiago cheese	1 1/2 cups	375 mL
Finely chopped green onion	2 tbsp.	30 mL

Heat butter and cooking oil in large frying pan on medium-low until butter
is melted. Add next 3 ingredients. Cook for about 25 minutes, stirring
occasionally, until onion is caramelized.

Combine pumpkin and sage in small bowl. Spread over pizza crust, almost
to edge. Scatter onion mixture over pumpkin mixture.

Sprinkle with cheese. Cook in 450°F (230°C) oven for about 15 minutes
until crust is golden and cheese is melted.

Sprinkle with green onion. Cuts into 16 wedges.

*1 wedge: 76 Calories; 5.2 g Total Fat (0.7 g Mono, 0.3 g Poly, 2.4 g Sat); 11 mg Cholesterol;
5 g Carbohydrate; 1 g Fibre; 3 g Protein; 161 mg Sodium*

sunnyside pizza

Move over breakfast sandwich, breakfast pizza has arrived! The whole family will love this dish.

Prebaked pizza crust (6 inch, 15 cm, diameter)	1	1
Mild (or medium) salsa	3 tbsp.	45 mL
Grated medium (or mild) Cheddar cheese	2 tbsp.	30 mL
Bacon slices, cooked almost crisp and diced	3	3
Tomato slices	3	3
Large egg	1	1
Grated medium (or mild) Cheddar cheese	3 tbsp.	45 mL

Place pizza crust on ungreased baking sheet. Spread salsa evenly on crust, almost to edge. Sprinkle first amount of cheese over salsa, leaving 2 to 3 inch (5 to 7.5 cm) circle in centre bare of cheese. Scatter bacon over cheese. Arrange tomato slices over bacon. Break egg into circle. Sprinkle second amount of cheese over egg. Bake in 450°F (230°C) oven for about 15 minutes until crust is crisp and egg is set. Cuts into 4 wedges.

1 wedge: 132 Calories; 7.2 g Total Fat (2.5 g Mono, 0.6 g Poly, 3.1 g Sat); 67 mg Cholesterol; 10 g Carbohydrate; trace Fibre; 7 g Protein; 266 mg Sodium

g'morning pizza

This tasty pizza was a huge hit in our test kitchen—it disappeared in less than five minutes! A breakfast the whole family will enjoy, this dish is easy and quick to prepare. It is also a good choice for diabetics.

Large hard-boiled eggs, peeled	6	6
Light cream cheese	4 oz.	125 g
Parsley flakes	1/2 tsp.	2 mL
Dried sweet basil	1/2 tsp.	2 mL
Garlic powder	1/16 tsp.	0.5 mL
Premade pizza crust, 12 inch (30 cm)	1	1
Fat-free ham slices, diced	2/3 cup	150 mL
Grated part-skim mozzarella cheese	1 cup	250 mL
Thinly sliced red onion	1/2 cup	125 mL
Thinly sliced green and red peppers	2/3 cup	150 mL
Dried sweet basil, sprinkle (optional)		
Dried whole oregano, sprinkle (optional)		

Discard 4 yolks. Chop remaining egg whites and 2 whole eggs.

Combine next 4 ingredients in small bowl. Spread onto crust. Layer with eggs and next 4 ingredients, in order. Sprinkle with basil and oregano. Bake in centre of 400°F (200°C) oven for 8 to 10 minutes until cheese is melted and crust is browned. Cuts into 8 wedges.

1 wedge: 230 Calories; 11 g Total Fat (2 g Mono, 0.5 g Poly, 5 g Sat); 185 mg Cholesterol; 19 g Carbohydrate; < 1 g Fibre; 14 g Protein; 460 mg Sodium

peppy personal pizzas

This thin-crust pizza with colourful veggie toppings smothered in tangy cheese makes a simple but delightful lunch.

Flour tortillas (9 inch, 22 cm, diameter)	4	4
Can of pizza sauce (7 1/2 oz., 213 mL), or simple pizza sauce, page 2	1	1
Sliced fresh white mushrooms	3/4 cup	175 mL
Thinly sliced red pepper	3/4 cup	175 mL
Thinly sliced green pepper	3/4 cup	175 mL
Thinly sliced red onion	1/2 cup	125 mL
Crumbled feta cheese (about 5 oz., 140 g)	1 cup	250 mL
Grated havarti cheese	1 cup	250 mL

Preheat oven to 425°F (220°C). Place tortillas on 2 greased baking sheets. Spread pizza sauce evenly on each tortilla.

Divide and layer remaining 6 ingredients, in order given, on top of sauce. Bake on separate racks in oven for about 15 minutes, switching position of baking sheets at halftime, until cheese is melted and edges are golden. Makes 4 pizzas.

1 pizza: 423 Calories; 22.1 g Total Fat (6.5 g Mono, 2.4 g Poly, 12 g Sat); 67 mg Cholesterol; 39 g Carbohydrate; 3 g Fibre; 19g Protein; 1146 mg Sodium

pizza on the grill

You haven't had pizza until you've had it made on the barbecue!

Biscuit mix	2 cups	500 mL
Milk	1/2 cup	125 mL
Simple pizza sauce, page 2	1 cup	250 mL
Grated part-skim mozzarella cheese	2 cups	500 mL
Sliced fresh white mushrooms	1 cup	250 mL
Chopped deli meat (your favourite)	1 cup	250 mL
Chopped green onion	1/2 cup	125 mL
Chopped red pepper	1/2 cup	125 mL
Grated part-skim mozzarella cheese	1 cup	250 mL

Measure biscuit mix into medium bowl. Add milk. Stir until just moistened. Turn out dough onto lightly floured surface. Knead 8 to 10 times. Press evenly in greased 12 inch (30 cm) pizza pan. Preheat barbecue to high. Place pan on 1 side of ungreased grill. Turn off burner under pan, turning opposite burner down to medium. Close lid. Cook for about 15 minutes, rotating pan at halftime, until crust is just starting to turn golden.

Spread pizza sauce evenly over crust. Layer next 5 ingredients, in order given, over sauce. Sprinkle with second amount of mozzarella cheese. Return to unlit side of grill. Close lid. Cook for about 15 minutes until heated through and cheese is melted. Cuts into 6 wedges.

1 wedge: 481 Calories; 22.9 g Total Fat (8.1 g Mono, 4 g Poly, 9.3 g Sat); 57 mg Cholesterol; 41 g Carbohydrate; 1 g Fibre; 27 g Protein; 1560 mg Sodium

pesto pita pizzas

Quick and simple! Pesto and olives give these pita pizzas their pizzazz, and turkey gives them their protein. Fit for the whole family.

Pita breads (7 inch, 18 cm, diameter)	4	4
Sun-dried tomato pesto	8 tsp.	40 mL
Crumbled light feta cheese	1 cup	250 mL
Chopped deli turkey breast slices	1 cup	250 mL
Chopped kalamata olives	1/4 cup	60 mL
Chopped tomato	1 cup	250 mL
Dried basil	2 tsp.	10 mL

Preheat oven to 400°F (200°C). Arrange pitas on 2 baking sheets. Spread 2 tsp. (10 mL) pesto on each pita. Layer next 4 ingredients, in order given, over pesto. Sprinkle basil over top. Bake on separate racks in oven for about 10 minutes, switching position of baking sheets at halftime, until pitas are crisp and cheese is melted. Serves 4.

1 serving: *349 Calories; 8.4 g Total Fat (0.8 g Mono, 0.5 g Poly, 4.3 g Sat); 46 mg Cholesterol; 42 g Carbohydrate; 2 g Fibre; 30 g Protein; 1853 mg Sodium*

pizza pockets

Pizza in a perfect little package! These pockets freeze well—ideal for lunch at school or the office.

Lean ground chicken (or beef or pork)	8 oz.	225 g
Chopped onion	1 cup	250 mL
Garlic clove, minced	1	1
Grated zucchini, with peel	1 cup	250 mL
Can of regular tomato sauce (71/2 oz., 213 mL)	1	1
Dried oregano	1/2 tsp.	2 mL
Dried basil	1 tsp.	5 mL
Dried crushed chilies	1/8 tsp.	0.5 mL
Grated part-skim mozzarella cheese	3/4 cup	175 mL
Grated Parmesan cheese	2 tbsp.	30 mL
Whole wheat flour	2/3 cup	150 mL
All-purpose flour	1 cup	250 mL
Baking powder	4 tsp.	20 mL
Salt	1/2 tsp.	2 mL
Canola oil	3 tbsp.	45 mL
Skim milk	3/4 cup	175 mL
All-purpose flour	1/3 cup	75 mL
Skim milk	1/4 cup	60 mL

Sauté first 4 ingredients in large non-stick frying pan until no pink remains in chicken and liquid is evaporated.

Stir in next 4 ingredients. Heat, uncovered, for 10 minutes on low, stirring occasionally, until thickened. Remove from heat. Let stand to cool slightly. Stir in both cheeses.

Combine whole wheat flour, first amount of all-purpose flour, baking powder and salt in medium bowl. Make a well in centre.

Combine canola oil and first amount of milk in small bowl. Add, all at once, to dry ingredients. Stir with fork just until moistened. Turn out and gently knead dough on floured surface, using second amount of all-purpose flour, about 8 to 10 times. Divide dough into 8 portions. Roll each out to 6 inch (15 cm) circle. Place 1/3 cup (75 mL) filling to one side of centre. Moisten edge of dough with some of second amount of milk. Bring unfilled side of dough over filling and press edges together with fork tines to seal well. Cut 3 or 4 slits in top with tip of sharp knife. Place on greased baking sheet. Brush with remaining milk. Bake in 400°F (200°C) oven for 13 to15 minutes until golden brown. Makes 8 pockets.

1 pocket: 250 Calories; 9 g Total Fat (4 g Mono, 1.5 g Poly, 2.5 g Sat); 30 mg Cholesterol; 30 g Carbohydrate; 3 g Fibre; 14 g Protein; 540 mg Sodium

pizza in disguise

These golden half moons of pastry are filled with a mild pizza mixture.

Olive (or cooking) oil	1 tbsp.	15 mL
Finely chopped onion	1/2 cup	125 mL
Garlic clove, minced (or 1/4 tsp., 1 mL, powder)	1	1
Finely chopped green pepper	1/2 cup	125 mL
Pizza sauce	1/2 cup	125 mL
Chopped deli salami (or ham) slices (about 4 oz., 113 g)	3/4 cup	175 mL
Grated part-skim mozzarella cheese	1 cup	250 mL
Frozen dough dinner rolls, thawed but not risen	8	8
Large egg, fork-beaten	1	1

Heat olive oil in large frying pan on medium. Add onion, garlic and green pepper. Cook, stirring often, until onion is softened. Turn into large bowl. Cool.

Add next 3 ingredients. Mix well.

Roll out each dinner roll on lightly floured surface to about 6 inch (15 cm) circle. Spread 1/4 cup (60 mL) filling on 1/2 of each circle, leaving 1/2 inch (12 mm) edge. Fold other halves of dough over filling. Press edges together with fork to seal well. Place on greased baking sheet.

Brush tops and sides with egg. Bake in 375°F (190°C) oven for about 20 minutes until golden brown. Let stand on baking sheet for 5 minutes before removing to serving plate. Serve warm. Makes 8 calzones.

1 calzone: 215 Calories; 11.4 g Total Fat (5.3 g Mono, 1.2 g Poly, 4.2 g Sat); 49 mg Cholesterol; 20 g Carbohydrate; 1 g Fibre; 9 g Protein; 446 mg Sodium

greek salad pizza

Colourful, Greek-style toppings on a knife-and-fork pizza. Serve with lemon wedges to squeeze over top for an extra splash of flavour.

Cooking oil	1 tsp.	5 mL
Lean ground beef	1/2 lb.	225 g
Chopped onion	1/2 cup	125 mL
Garlic clove, minced	1	1
Box of frozen chopped spinach (10 oz., 300 g), thawed and squeezed dry	1	1
Dried oregano	1 tsp.	5 mL
Prebaked pizza crust (12 inch, 30 cm, diameter)	1	1
Simple pizza sauce, page 2	1/4 cup	60 mL
Grated part-skim mozzarella cheese	1 cup	250 mL
Can of sliced ripe olives, drained (4 1/2 oz., 125 mL)	1	1
Crumbled feta cheese	1 cup	250 mL
Chopped tomato	1 cup	250 mL
Chopped fresh mint leaves (optional)	1 tbsp.	15 mL

Heat cooking oil in medium frying pan on medium. Add ground beef, onion and garlic. Scramble-fry for about 10 minutes until beef is no longer pink. Drain.

Add spinach and oregano. Heat and stir for 2 minutes.

Place pizza crust on ungreased baking sheet. Spread pizza sauce on crust. Scatter beef mixture over sauce. Sprinkle with mozzarella cheese. Bake in 450°F (230°C) oven for about 10 minutes until crust is golden and cheese is melted and starting to brown.

Scatter remaining 4 ingredients, in order given, over top. Cuts into 8 wedges.

1 wedge: 258 Calories; 12 g Total Fat (3.7 g Mono, 0.7 g Poly, 5.7 g Sat); 42 mg Cholesterol; 22 g Carbohydrate; 2 g Fibre; 16 g Protein; 590 mg Sodium

orzo crust pizza

A unique pizza using orzo pasta as the crust.

Orzo	1 cup	250 mL
Boiling water	4 cups	1 L
Salt	1 tsp.	5 mL
Frozen egg product, thawed	6 tbsp.	100 mL
Grated Parmesan cheese	2 tbsp.	30 mL
Parsley flakes	2 tsp.	10 mL
Tomato sauce	1 1/2 cups	375 mL
Lean ground beef	1/2 lb.	225 g
Seasoning salt	1/2 tsp.	2 mL
Pepper	1/4 tsp.	1 mL
Dried oregano	1/2 tsp.	2 mL
Medium green or red pepper, cut into rings	1	1
Medium red onion, thinly sliced	1/2	1/2
Chopped fresh mushrooms	2/3 cup	150 mL
Grated part-skim mozzarella cheese	1 cup	250 mL

Cook orzo in boiling water and salt in large saucepan for 12 to 15 minutes, stirring occasionally, until tender but firm. Drain. Return to saucepan.

Combine egg product, Parmesan cheese and parsley in small bowl. Mix. Pour over hot pasta. Toss well. Press in greased 12 inch (30 cm) deep dish pizza pan, forming a crust. Spread tomato sauce over top almost to edges.

Scramble-fry ground beef, breaking up any large chunks, in medium non-stick skillet until no longer pink. Drain. Add seasoning salt, pepper and oregano. Stir.

Scatter beef over tomato sauce. Cover with green pepper, onion and mushrooms. Sprinkle mozzarella cheese over top. Bake in 400°F (200°C) oven for 20 minutes until cheese is melted and edges are golden. Cuts into 8 wedges.

1 wedge: 210 Calories; 7 g Total Fat (2.5 g Mono, 0 g Poly, 3.5 g Sat); 30 mg Cholesterol; 20 g Carbohydrate; 2 g Fibre; 10 g Protein; 790 mg Sodium

ham tomato pizza

Tastes like a ham and tomato sandwich—only better! Colourful and inviting.

Prebaked pizza crust (12 inch, 30 cm, diameter)	1	1
Grated medium (or mild) Cheddar cheese	1/2 cup	125 mL
Diced cooked ham	1 cup	250 mL
Finely chopped celery	2/3 cup	150 mL
Salad dressing (or mayonnaise)	1/4 cup	60 mL
Sliced green onion	1/4 cup	60 mL
Seasoned salt	1/4 tsp.	1 mL
Medium tomatoes, thinly sliced	2	2
Grated medium (or mild) Cheddar cheese	3/4 cup	175 mL
Salad dressing (or mayonnaise)	1/3 cup	75 mL

Place pizza crust on ungreased 12 inch (30 cm) pizza pan. Sprinkle crust with first amount of cheese.

Combine next 5 ingredients in small bowl. Spoon onto cheese. Spread evenly. Bake in 450°F (230°C) oven for 10 to 15 minutes until crust is crisp and golden.

Arrange tomato slices in single layer over ham mixture.

Combine second amounts of cheese and salad dressing in separate small bowl. Divide and spoon cheese mixture onto each tomato slice. Flatten cheese mixture slightly with back of spoon. Broil 6 inches (15 cm) from heat in oven for 3 to 4 minutes until crust starts to brown and cheese is melted. Cuts into 8 wedges.

1 wedge: 295 Calories; 18 g Total Fat (7.5 g Mono, 3.4 g Poly, 5.2 g Sat); 35 mg Cholesterol; 21 g Carbohydrate; 1 g Fibre; 13 g Protein; 730 mg Sodium

rice crust pizza pie

A cheese-covered pizza with bright peppers and lots of flavour makes this a good choice for using up that leftover rice. The edges of the moist rice base turn crisp and golden in the oven. Delicious!

Large egg	1	1
Leftover cooked rice	1 1/2 cups	375 mL
Grated part-skim mozzarella cheese	1/2 cup	125 mL
Grated Parmesan cheese	1 tbsp.	15 mL
Pizza (or spaghetti) sauce	1/3 cup	75 mL
Thinly sliced pepperoni	1/2 cup	125 mL
Sliced fresh white mushrooms	1/2 cup	125 mL
Chopped green pepper	1/4 cup	60 mL
Grated part-skim mozzarella cheese	1 cup	250 mL
Slivered red, green or yellow pepper	1/2 cup	125 mL

Beat egg with fork in small bowl. Add rice, first amount of mozzarella cheese and Parmesan cheese. Stir until combined. Spread in greased 9 inch (23 cm) pie plate, building up side slightly. Pack down well. Bake in 450°F (230°C) oven for 10 to 12 minutes until edge is starting to brown.

Spread pizza sauce in even layer over crust. Layer pepperoni, mushrooms and green pepper in order given over sauce. Scatter second amount of mozzarella cheese and slivered pepper over top. Bake, uncovered, in 450°F (230°C) oven for about 10 minutes until edge is browned and cheese is melted. Let stand in pie plate for 5 minutes. Cuts into 4 wedges.

1 wedge: 428 Calories; 22.9 g Total Fat (9.2 g Mono, 2 g Poly, 10.2 g Sat); 101 mg Cholesterol; 31 g Carbohydrate; 1 g Fibre; 23 g Protein; 953 mg Sodium

thai pizza on a garlic crust

A thin crust pizza with lots of colour and crunch from the fresh vegetables.

All-purpose flour, approximately	1 1/3 cups	325 mL
Instant yeast	1 tsp.	5 mL
Salt	1/2 tsp.	2 mL
Garlic powder	1/4 tsp.	1 mL
Hot water	1/2 cup	125 mL
Cooking oil	1 tbsp.	15 mL
Peanut sauce	1/4 cup	60 mL
Grated part-skim mozzarella cheese	3/4 cup	175 mL
Boneless, skinless chicken breast half cut into 1/8 inch (3 mm) slices	6 oz.	170 g
Medium carrot, cut julienne	1	1
Cayenne pepper	1/8 tsp.	0.5 mL
Cooking (or chili-flavoured) oil	1 tbsp.	15 mL
Large red pepper, cut into 8 rings	1	1
Fresh bean sprouts	1 cup	250 mL
Green onions, sliced diagonally	3	3
Sesame seeds, toasted (see Tip, page 64)	1 tsp.	5 mL

Combine first 4 ingredients in medium bowl. Add hot water and first amount of cooking oil. Mix well until dough pulls away from sides of bowl. Turn out onto lightly floured surface. Knead for 5 to 8 minutes until smooth and elastic. Cover with tea towel. Let dough rest for 15 minutes.

Roll out and press into greased 12 inch (30 cm) pizza pan, forming rim around edge. Spread with peanut sauce. Sprinkle with cheese.

Sauté chicken, carrot and cayenne pepper in second amount of cooking oil in frying pan for about 5 minutes until chicken is no longer pink. Arrange over cheese. Place red pepper around outside edge. Bake on bottom rack in 425°F (220°C) oven for 15 minutes until cheese is melted and crust is golden. Remove from oven. Sprinkle with bean sprouts, green onion and sesame seeds. Cuts into 8 wedges.

1 wedge: 200 Calories; 8 g Total Fat (3 g Mono, 1 g Poly, 2 g Sat); 25 mg Cholesterol; 21 g Carbohydrate; 1 g Fibre; 11 g Protein; 350 mg Sodium

stuffed-crust pizza

The puffy cheese-filled crust will make this pizza a favourite.

Very warm water	1 1/4 cups	300 mL
Granulated sugar	1 tsp.	5 mL
Olive (or cooking) oil	1 tbsp.	15 mL
Salt	1 tsp.	5 mL
All-purpose flour, approximately	1 1/2 cups	375 mL
Instant yeast (or 1/4 oz., 8 g, envelope)	2 1/4 tsp.	11 mL
All-purpose flour	1 1/2 cups	375 mL
Mozzarella cheese sticks	7	7
Basil pesto	3 tbsp.	45 mL
Diced cooked chicken	1 cup	250 mL
Grated mozzarella cheese	1 1/2 cups	375 mL
Roasted red pepper, cut into strips	1	1
Thinly sliced red onion rings	1/2 cup	125 mL
Freshly grated Romano cheese	3 tbsp.	45 mL
Fresh tomato slices (about 1 large)	8	8

Stir first 4 ingredients together in medium bowl until sugar is dissolved.

Combine first amount of flour and yeast in small bowl. Stir into water mixture until smooth.

Work in enough of second amount of flour until dough is no longer sticky. Turn out onto lightly floured surface. Knead for 2 minutes. Cover. Let stand for 15 minutes. Roll out into 13 inch (33 cm) circle and press in greased 12 inch (30 cm) pizza pan, letting excess dough drape over edge. Roll up cheese sticks in excess dough all around edge. Pinch edge to base of crust to seal.

Spread pesto on crust just to beginning of rolled crust. Cover with waxed paper. Let stand in oven with light on and door closed for 30 minutes until doubled in size.

Layer next 5 ingredients on crust in order given. Bake on center rack in 450°F (230°C) oven for 15 to 20 minutes until cheese is melted and crust is browned. Arrange tomato slices on top. Cuts into 8 wedges.

1 wedge: 410 Calories; 17 g Total Fat (3.3 g Mono, 1 g Poly, 8 g Sat); 45 mg Cholesterol; 41 g Carbohydrate; 2 g Fibre; 22 g Protein; 940 mg Sodium

springtime chicken pizza

This cheesy chicken pizza, topped with lots of veggies, is destined to become a year-round favourite.

Prebaked pizza crust (12 inch, 30 cm, diameter)	1	1
Simple pizza sauce, page 2	1/3 cup	75 mL
Grated Parmesan cheese	1/2 cup	125 mL
Chopped cooked chicken	1 1/2 cups	375 mL
Roasted red peppers, drained, blotted dry, cut into strips	1/3 cup	75 mL
Fresh asparagus spears, trimmed of tough ends	8	8
Goat (chèvre) cheese, cut up	2/3 cup	150 mL

Preheat oven to 450°F (230°C). Place pizza crust on greased 12 inch (30 cm) pizza pan. Spread pizza sauce evenly on crust. Sprinkle with Parmesan cheese. Scatter chicken and red pepper over Parmesan cheese. Arrange asparagus spears in spoke pattern on top of red pepper. Scatter goat cheese over top. Bake for about 15 minutes until crust is crisp and golden. Cuts into 8 wedges.

1 wedge: 246 Calories; 10.5 g Total Fat (2.7 g Mono, 0.8 g Poly, 5.2 g Sat); 43 mg Cholesterol; 19 g Carbohydrate; 1 g Fibre; 18 g Protein; 455 mg Sodium

feta chicken pizza

Scrumptious sun-dried tomato and smoky bacon add to the unique combination of flavours on this crispy, golden pizza.

Basic pizza crust dough, page 2	1	1
Sun-dried tomato pesto	1/3 cup	75 mL
Whipping cream (or whole milk)	1/4 cup	60 mL
Chopped cooked chicken	1 1/2 cups	375 mL
Bacon slices, cooked crisp and crumbled	4	4
Chopped green pepper	1/2 cup	125 mL
Pine nuts, toasted (see Tip, page 64)	1/3 cup	75 mL
Chopped fresh basil (or 1 1/2 tsp., 7 mL, dried)	2 tbsp.	30 mL
Crumbled feta cheese (about 4 1/2 oz., 126 g)	2/3 cup	150 mL
Finely grated Parmesan cheese	1/2 cup	125 mL

Prepare pizza dough. Roll out and press in greased 12 inch (30 cm) pizza pan, forming rim around edge.

Combine pesto and whipping cream in small bowl. Spread on crust.

Top with remaining 7 ingredients. Bake in 450°F (230°C) oven for 15 to 18 minutes until cheese is melted and crust is browned. Cuts into 6 wedges.

1 wedge: 500 Calories; 28 g Total Fat (9 g Mono, 4.5 g Poly, 9 g Sat); 70 mg Cholesterol; 37 g Carbohydrate; 2 g Fibre; 25 g Protein; 1070 mg Sodium

salmon and goat cheese pizza

Put a sophisticated spin on your next pizza. Goat cheese, smoked salmon, lemon zest and Kalamata olives make for an unexpected, but totally uptown twist on tradition!

Goat (chèvre) cheese, cut up	4 oz.	113 g
Unbaked pizza crust (12 inch, 30 cm diameter)	1	1
Chopped red onion	1/4 cup	60 mL
Grated lemon zest	1 tbsp.	15 mL
Chopped smoked salmon slices (about 4 oz., 113 g)	2/3 cup	150 mL
Kalamata olives, pitted and halved	1/4 cup	60 mL

Scatter cheese over pizza crust. Combine onion and lemon zest in small bowl. Sprinkle over cheese. Bake in 450°F (230°C) oven for about 10 minutes until crust is golden brown.

Arrange smoked salmon over top. Sprinkle with olives. Cuts into 8 wedges.

1 wedge: 102 Calories; 4.8 g Total Fat (1.3 g Mono, 0.3 g Poly, 2.3 g Sat); 10 mg Cholesterol; 9 g Carbohydrate; 1 g Fibre; 7 g Protein; 263 mg Sodium

tuna melt pizza

Combines the popular flavours of pizza and tuna melt sandwiches into a new family-friendly hit. Also good for lunch the next day.

Prebaked multi-grain (or whole wheat) pizza crust (12 inch, 30 cm, diameter)	1	1
Alfredo pasta sauce	1/2 cup	125 mL
Can of chunk light tuna in water (6 oz., 170 g), drained	1	1
Finely chopped red onion	1/4 cup	60 mL
Diced red pepper	2/3 cup	150 mL
Finely chopped celery	1/3 cup	75 mL
Grated Swiss cheese	1 cup	250 mL
Diced seeded tomato	1/2 cup	125 mL
Chopped fresh parsley	1 tbsp.	15 mL

Place crust on ungreased 12 inch (30 cm) pizza pan.

Combine next 3 ingredients in small bowl. Spread over crust.

Scatter next 3 ingredients, in order given, over tuna mixture. Bake in 450°F (230°C) oven for about 15 minutes until crust is browned.

Sprinkle with tomato and parsley. Cuts into 8 wedges.

1 wedge: *170 Calories; 6 g Total Fat (0 g Mono, 0 g Poly, 3 g Sat); 24 mg Cholesterol; 18 g Carbohydrate; 2 g Fibre; 11 g Protein; 338 mg Sodium*

pizza margherita

This pizza represents the colours of the Italian flag—green basil, red sauce and white cheese. For a more rustic appearance, trying pressing out the dough instead of rolling.

Tomato sauce	1/4 cup	60 mL
Balsamic vinegar	1 tsp.	5 mL
Partially baked 12 inch (30 cm) whole wheat pizza crust	1	1
Regular bocconcini (fresh mozzarella), about 2 inch (5 cm) diameter, sliced 1/4 inch (6 mm) thick (see Tip, page 64)	4	4
Salt, sprinkle		
Pepper, sprinkle		
Chopped fresh basil	2 tbsp.	30 mL

Combine tomato sauce and vinegar in small bowl. Spread sauce mixture over crust to within 1/4 inch (6 mm) of edge.

Arrange cheese over top. Sprinkle with salt and pepper. Bake on bottom rack in 450°F (230°C) oven for about 15 minutes until crust is browned on bottom and cheese is starting to brown.

Sprinkle with basil. Let stand for 5 minutes. Cuts into 8 wedges.

1 wedge: 220 Calories; 10.0 g Total Fat (4.0 g Mono, 0.5 g Poly, 4.5 g Sat); 20 mg Cholesterol; 24 g Carbohydrate; 2 g Fibre; 9 g Protein; 440 mg Sodium

falafel pizza

An inspired take on a Middle Eastern specialty.

All-purpose flour	1 1/2 cups	375 mL
Whole wheat flour	1 cup	250 mL
Instant yeast	2 tsp.	10 mL
Salt	1/4 tsp.	1 mL
Granulated sugar	2 tsp.	10 mL
Toasted sesame seeds	2 tbsp.	30 mL
Hot water	1 cup	250 mL
Olive oil	2 tbsp.	30 mL
Chicken broth	1/2 cup	125 mL
Chopped onion	1 cup	250 mL
Garlic cloves, minced	3	3
Canned chickpeas (garbanzo beans), 19 oz., 540 mL, drained	1	1
Egg white (large)	1	1
Chopped fresh parsley	1 1/2 tbsp.	25 mL
Ground cumin	1/2 tsp.	2 mL
Ground coriander	3/4 tsp.	4 mL
Ground turmeric	1/8 tsp.	0.5 mL
Salt	1 tsp.	5 mL
Freshly ground pepper	1/8 tsp.	0.5 mL
Thin tomato slices	12	12
Thin green pepper rings	12	12
Thin red onion rings	12	12
Grated part-skim mozzarella cheese	1 cup	250 mL

Combine first 6 ingredients in medium bowl. Stir water and oil together in small cup. Add all at once to flour mixture, stirring with fork until combined and dough leaves sides of bowl. Turn out on lightly floured surface and knead about 30 times. Cover with bowl. Allow to rest for 10 minutes.

Heat broth in small saucepan. Add onion and garlic and cook for 7 to 8 minutes until soft.

Add next 8 ingredients to food processor. Process to combine. Add broth mixture and process until almost smooth.

Lightly grease flat working surface. Roll out dough and fit in lightly greased 14 inch (35 cm) pizza pan, making slightly raised edge all around. Spread chickpea mixture over crust. Bake in 425°F (220°C) oven, on centre rack for 15 minutes. Top with tomato slices, pepper rings and red onion rings. Sprinkle with mozzarella cheese. Bake for 15 minutes until cheese is lightly browned. Cuts into 8 wedges.

1 wedge: 310 Calories; 10 g Total Fat (4 g Mono, 1 g Poly, 3 g Sat); 35 mg Cholesterol; 45 g Carbohydrate; 6 g Fibre; 1 2g Protein; 660 mg Sodium

pepper quinoa pizza

This distinctive, delicious quinoa crust is packed with protein and is gluten free.

Prepared vegetable broth	1 3/4 cups	425 mL
Quinoa, rinsed and drained	1 1/4 cups	300 mL
Cornstarch	1/4 cup	60 mL
Basil pesto	2 tbsp.	30 mL
Canola oil	2 tbsp.	30 mL
Yellow cornmeal	2 tbsp.	30 mL
Tomato sauce	1/2 cup	125 mL
Thinly sliced fresh white mushrooms	1 cup	250 mL
Diced red pepper	1 cup	250 mL
Diced yellow pepper	1 cup	250 mL
Grated Asiago cheese	3/4 cup	175 mL

Bring broth to a boil in medium saucepan. Add quinoa. Stir. Reduce heat to medium-low. Simmer, covered, for about 20 minutes, without stirring, until quinoa is tender and liquid is absorbed. Spread on large plate to cool. Transfer to food processor.

Add next three ingredients. Process until combined and mixture resembles dough.

Sprinkle cornmeal over well-greased 12 inch (30 cm) pizza pan. Press quinoa mixture into pan. Bake on bottom rack in 450°F (230°C) oven for about 15 minutes until set and edges are dry.

Spread tomato sauce over crust. Scatter remaining 4 ingredients, in order given, over tomato sauce. Bake for about 20 minutes until cheese is melted and golden. Cuts into 8 wedges.

1 wedge: 230 Calories; 12 g Total Fat (2 g Mono, 1 g Poly, 3.5 g Sat); 15 mg Cholesterol; 24 g Carbohydrate; 2 g Fibre; 7 g Protein; 410 mg Sodium

rosti pizza

Potato and celery root form the crust of this tasty pizza, which is topped with lots of herb flavour and a mild chili heat.

Grated celery root	1 3/4 cups	425 mL
Grated peeled potato	1 3/4 cups	425 mL
Finely chopped onion	1/2 cup	125 mL
Large egg, fork-beaten	1	1
All-purpose flour	1/4 cup	60 mL
Cooking oil	1 tbsp.	15 mL
Dried rosemary, crushed	1/2 tsp.	2 mL
Salt	1/2 tsp.	2 mL
Pepper	1/4 tsp.	1 mL
Cooking oil	2 tbsp.	30 mL
Tomato sauce	1/4 cup	60 mL
Sun-dried tomato pesto	2 tbsp.	30 mL
Dried crushed chilies	1/4 tsp.	1 mL
Grated Italian cheese blend	1 cup	250 mL
Large tomato slices, halved	4	4
Chopped fresh basil	2 tsp.	10 mL

Place first 3 ingredients in fine sieve. Let stand over medium bowl for 15 minutes. Squeeze celery root mixture to remove excess moisture. Transfer to large bowl. Add next 6 ingredients. Mix well.

Heat 1 tbsp. (15 mL) cooking oil in large non-stick frying pan on medium. Spoon celery root mixture into pan. Press down lightly to cover bottom of pan. Cook for about 10 minutes until bottom is crisp and golden. Slide onto plate. Heat remaining cooking oil in same frying pan. Invert celery root mixture onto another plate. Slide into pan, golden side up. Cook for about 5 minutes until bottom is crisp and golden.

Combine next 3 ingredients in small bowl. Spread over celery root mixture, almost to edge. Sprinkle with cheese. Broil on centre rack in oven for about 2 minutes until cheese is melted (see Tip, page 64). Transfer to cutting board. Arrange tomato slices over top. Sprinkle with basil. Cuts into 8 wedges. Serve immediately. Serves 4.

1 serving: 330 Calories; 19 g Total Fat (7 g Mono, 3 g Poly, 4.5 g Sat); 55 mg Cholesterol; 28 g Carbohydrate; 3 g Fibre; 11 g Protein; 660 mg Sodium

apple and cheese pizza

A very pretty presentation for dessert. Try it for brunch or lunch too!

All-purpose flour	1 cup	250 mL
Whole wheat flour	1/2 cup	125 mL
Instant yeast	1 1/2 tsp.	7 mL
Salt	1/2 tsp.	2 mL
Granulated sugar	1/4 tsp.	1 mL
Ground cinnamon	1/4 tsp.	1 mL
Canola oil	2 tbsp.	30 mL
Very warm water	1/2 cup	125 mL
Red apples, with peel, cored and thinly sliced	2	2
Lemon juice	1/2 cup	125 mL
Grated sharp Cheddar cheese	1 cup	250 mL
Brown sugar, packed	1/4 cup	60 mL

Measure first 6 ingredients into food processor. Process briefly to combine.

Pour oil and very warm water through opening in lid while processing, until dough starts to form a ball. Knead 4 or 5 times on lightly floured surface. Cover. Let rest in warm place for 15 minutes. Divide ball into 4 equal portions. Pat or roll out each into thin 7 inch (18 cm) circle. Cover.

Place apple in medium bowl. Let stand in lemon juice until ready to use.

Preheat lightly sprayed electric grill to high. Place 1 crust on grill. Cover with large saucepan lid. Cook each crust for 2 to 3 minutes until bottom is crisp and "spotty." Turn over. Cover browned sides with cheese. Drain apple and blot dry. Divide and arrange over cheese. Sprinkle each with about 1 tbsp. (15 mL) brown sugar. Cover with lid. Cook for 2 to 3 minutes until cheese is melted and bottom of crust is browned. Makes 4 pizzas.

1 pizza: 460 Calories; 17 g Total Fat (7 g Mono, 2.5 g Poly, 7 g Sat); 30 mg Cholesterol; 67 g Carbohydrate; 6 g Fibre; g 13 Protein; 480 mg Sodium

triple chocolate pizza

The photo says it all!

All-purpose flour	2 cups	500 mL
Granulated sugar	1 1/4 cups	300 mL
Cocoa, sifted	1/3 cup	75 mL
Hard margarine, softened	3/4 cup	175 mL
Large eggs, fork-beaten	2	2
Cream cheese, softened	8 oz.	250 g
Granulated sugar	3/4 cup	175 mL
Large egg	1	1
Cocoa, sifted	1/4 cup	60 mL
Vanilla	1 tsp.	5 mL
Semisweet chocolate chips	1/3 cup	75 mL
White chocolate chips	1/3 cup	75 mL
Butterscotch chips	1/3 cup	75 mL
Maraschino cherries, drained and halved	8	8
Sliced almonds	1 tbsp.	15 mL

For the crust, measure flour, sugar and cocoa into bowl. Add margarine. Cut in until crumbly.

Add eggs. Mix well. Press in greased 12 inch (30 cm) pizza pan. Bake in 350°F (175°C) oven for 15 minutes.

For the filling, beat next 5 ingredients together until smooth. Spread over hot crust. Return to oven for 10 minutes.

Sprinkle with 3 kinds of chips. Let stand until soft. Draw tip of knife back and forth over top to smooth out most of the chips. If necessary, return to warm oven for a minute.

Place cherries here and there. Place almond slices around edge. Cool. Cuts into 12 wedges.

1 wedge: 480 Calories; 24 g Total Fat (6 g Mono, 4 g Poly, 10 g Sat); 75 mg Cholesterol; 63 g Carbohydrate; 3 g Fibre; 7 g Protein; 220 mg Sodium

crispy fruit pizza

A dessert pizza you can eat with your fingers. This is amazing! It can be made the day before but do not freeze.

Butter (or hard margarine)	1/4 cup	60 mL
Large marshmallows	32	32
Crisp rice cereal	5 cups	1.25 L
Cream cheese, softened (at room temperature)	8 oz.	250 g
Icing (confectioner's) sugar	2 cups	500 mL
Cocoa	1/4 cup	60 mL
Small strawberries, halved, reserve 1 whole berry	16	16
Banana, peeled and sliced	1	1
Kiwi fruit, peeled, halved lengthwise and sliced	2	2
Apricot jam	2 tbsp.	30 mL
Water	1 1/2 tsp.	7 mL
Whipping cream	1 cup	250 mL
Granulated sugar	2 tsp.	10 mL
Vanilla extract	1/2 tsp.	2 mL

For crust, combine butter and marshmallows in saucepan on medium-low heat, stirring often, until melted. Remove saucepan from heat. Add cereal. Stir until well coated. Press cereal mixture evenly over greased pan with wet fingers. Set aside to cool.

Place cream cheese, icing sugar and cocoa in small bowl. Beat on low speed until moistened. Beat on medium speed until smooth. Spread over cooled pizza base.

Arrange strawberries, bananas and kiwi over cream cheese mixture.

Mix jam and water in cup. With pastry brush, dab fruit with jam mixture to glaze and to prevent fruit from turning brown.

Beat whipping cream, sugar and vanilla in medium bowl until thick. Put dabs on top of the pizza. Cuts into 8 wedges.

1 wedge: 490 Calories; 23 g Total Fat (4 g Mono, 0.5 g Poly, 14 g Sat); 70 mg Cholesterol; 69 g Carbohydrate; 2 g Fibre; 5 g Protein; 310 mg Sodium

recipe index

topical tips

Baking/broiling with a non-ovenproof pan:
When baking or broiling food in a frying pan with a handle that isn't ovenproof, wrap the handle in foil and keep it to the front of the oven, away from the element.

Canned pumpkin: Be careful to purchase the right type of canned pumpkin that your recipe calls for. Pure pumpkin is just that—pumpkin with nothing added. Pumpkin pie filling, on the other hand, is pumpkin that has been blended with sugar and spices.

Prebaking pizza crust: To use the basic pizza crust dough in a recipe that calls for a prebaked crust, bake the dough in a 450°F (230°C) oven for 8 to 10 minutes.

Slicing bocconcini: Use an egg slicer to get perfectly even slices of bocconcini. They can be difficult to slice because they are so soft and round.

Toasting nuts, seeds or coconut: When toasting nuts, seeds or coconut, cooking times will vary for each type of nut—so never toast them together. For small amounts, place ingredient in an ungreased shallow frying pan. Heat on medium for 3 to 5 minutes, stirring often, until golden. For larger amounts, spread ingredient evenly in an ungreased shallow pan. Bake in a 350°F (175°C) oven for 5 to 10 minutes, stirring or shaking often, until golden.

Toasting pine nuts: Pine nuts have a relatively high oil content and burn easily, so take care when toasting them.

Nutrition Information Guidelines

Each recipe is analyzed using the Canadian Nutrient File from Health Canada, which is based on the United States Department of Agriculture (USDA) Nutrient Database.

- If more than one ingredient is listed (such as "butter or hard margarine"), or if a range is given (1 – 2 tsp., 5 – 10 mL), only the first ingredient or first amount is analyzed.

- For meat, poultry and fish, the serving size per person is based on the recommended 4 oz. (113 g) uncooked weight (without bone), which is 2 – 3 oz. (57 – 85 g) cooked weight (without bone)—approximately the size of a deck of playing cards.

- Milk used is 1% M.F. (milk fat), unless otherwise stated.

- Cooking oil used is canola oil, unless otherwise stated.

- Ingredients indicating "sprinkle," "optional" or "for garnish" are not included in the nutrition information.

- The fat in recipes and combination foods can vary greatly depending on the sources and types of fats used in each specific ingredient. For these reasons, the count of saturated, monounsaturated and polyunsaturated fats may not add up to the total fat content.